MILFISH96

WEIRD
AND
WONDERFUL
FISH.

COLIN S. MILKINS

Thomson Learning
New York

WEIRD AND WONDERFUL

FISH
FROGS & TOADS
INSECTS
SNAKES

Cover: A cowfish from the Caribbean.

First published in the United States in 1993 by
Thomson Learning; 115 Fifth Avenue; New York, NY 10003

First published in 1991 by Wayland (Publishers) Limited
61 Western Road, Hove, East Sussex BN3 IJD, England

Library of Congress Cataloging-in-Publication Data

Milkins, Colin S.
    Fish / Colin Milkins.
      p. cm. — (Weird and wonderful)
    Originally published: Hove, East Sussex, England : Wayland, 1991.
    Includes bibliographical references and index.
    Summary: Describes the physiology, feeding habits, and habitat of
several distinctly different and unique species of fish.
      ISBN 1-56847-008-8
      √. Fishes—[Juvenile literature] [1. Fishes.] √ Title.
II. Series.
QL617.2.M55 1993
597—dc20   91-6726

Printed in the United States of America

CONTENTS

1. Odd ways of swimming

Most fish can swim quickly through the water by lashing their tails from side to side. The cowfish cannot swim that way. It has sheets of bone beneath its skin that make its body too stiff. The cowfish swims slowly but surely by quickly beating its **pectoral fins**. It does not need to swim very fast because it is very **poisonous** and no other fish would want to eat it.

The elephant trunk fish is another example of a fish that does not swim in the usual way. By sending a wave along its **dorsal fin**, the fish moves forward in one smooth glide. By reversing the direction of the wave, it can swim equally well backward too.

The frog fish is such an odd shape that it probably could not swim very well even if it wanted to. It has grown to look just like the knobby **sponges** around it. The frog fish creeps along on the little "toes" at the tips of its pectoral fins, which look just like little stubby arms.

Below Look at the picture. Can you see the outline of the frog fish?

Right This odd-looking long-horned cowfish is using its pectoral fins to swim.

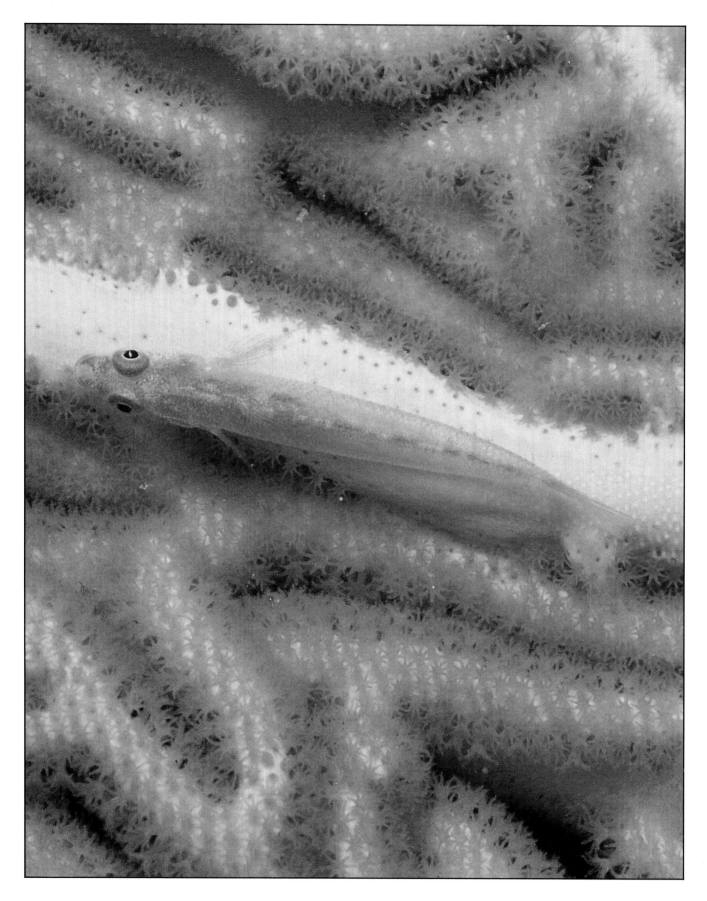

2. Biggest and smallest

The biggest fish in the oceans of the world is the massive whale shark. This huge creature can grow to over 42 ft (13 m) in length and weigh 23 tons. That is more than the weight of twenty cars. Although its mouth would be large enough for three men to crouch in, this "gentle giant" eats only tiny shrimp, called krill. These are strained from the sea water through special **gills** in the fish's mouth.

One of the smallest fish is the dwarf goby, which lives in the Indian Ocean. In length, it is also the smallest **vertebrate** known. An adult measures only 0.32 in (8 mm) —about the length of the nail on your little finger. No wonder fishermen do not bother to catch them.

There is another tiny goby that lives in freshwater lakes in the Philippines, in Southeast Asia. Fishermen do catch these, but they need to catch a lot because it takes more than 70,000 of them to make one fish cake!

Left This tiny goby lives on the coral of the Great Barrier Reef, in Australia.

Below The gentle whale shark would not harm the diver.

3. Unusual hunters

The archer fish lives in **mangrove swamps** and hunts insects it sees on the leaves above the water. Once an insect has been spotted, the archer fish quickly squeezes its gill covers. This sends a jet of water out of its mouth straight at the insect. The archer fish can spit very accurately, and usually the insect is knocked into the water. It will then be gobbled up by the archer fish.

The deep-sea angler fish also hunts in a strange way. Growing from its head is a feeler that acts like a "fishing rod." At the tip of the "rod" is a blob that glows with a greenish light.

This fish lives in deep, dark water and the light from the blob attracts the small fish that the deep-sea angler likes to eat. If a curious fish comes too close, the angler fish opens its mouth and sucks in the unlucky **prey**. This happens so quickly that the poor little fish just seems to vanish for no reason.

Below These two shrimp are getting too close to the deep-sea angler fish.

Right Archer fish can also leap out of the water to catch their prey.

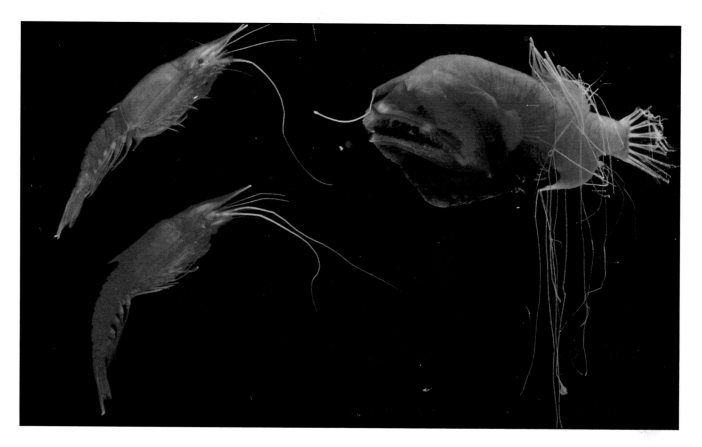

4. Shocking killers

The piranha is one of the fiercest of all fish. A **school** of over 100,000 piranha fish can easily overcome very large prey, using their razor-sharp teeth. A horse caught floundering in the water can be stripped of its flesh in a few minutes. Piranhas will sometimes eat humans too. In 1981, an overloaded ferry in Brazil, in South America, overturned, throwing 450 people into the water. In a feeding frenzy, a school of piranha ate 300 of them. But people in the water are not always attacked. Fishermen will often wade through water full of piranha. They come to no harm, because they avoid the usual piranha feeding times.

A truly "shocking" killer is the electric ray. This fish captures its prey by stunning it with an electric shock. Large rays could give a very nasty shock to a human too. Because it can give electric shocks, the ray can overcome large, fast-swimming fish that would otherwise be able to escape.

Left This picture shows the sharp teeth with which the piranha eats flesh.

Below The sting from an electric ray can cause a great deal of pain.

5. Crunchers and trappers

Lots of different fish live around **coral reefs**, but the parrot fish is one of the few that munches the coral itself. It does not actually eat the hard, chalky skeleton of the coral, but the tissue of the coral animals and the plants that live in it. The parrot fish's jaws, closed together, look just like the beak of a parrot, and they are excellent for crunching up coral. After feeding during the day, the parrot fish makes a cocoon around its body. It will sleep in this until morning.

Below Only clown fish are safe from the poisonous sting of the anemone.

The clown fish uses a poisonous sea anemone to protect itself and to trap food. The slime on the clown fish's body allows the fish to swim among the tentacles of the anemone without being stung. If the clown fish is chased by a larger fish it will plunge into the tentacles of the anemone for safety. If the larger fish continues to try to capture the clown fish, it will be stung to death by the anemone. The clown fish and the anemone will share the meal they have caught.

Right You can see how the parrot fish uses its "beak" to crunch the coral.

6. Blending in

When a flounder is lying flat on the ocean bed it is very difficult to see. This is because it can change the color of its spots to match the surroundings. If a flounder is resting on broken shells, some of the spots will turn white. If the fish then swims to a more sandy seabed, the spots turn yellow.

When resting, the flounder waggles its fins gently for a while to disturb the sand or shells. It does this so that the sand and shells settle on the edges of its body and hide its outline, making the fish even more difficult to see. The seal is one animal clever enough to find the flounder and eat it.

The leafy sea dragon is an Australian fish that **predators** also overlook. The fins of this strange-looking fish are long and straggly. When they are swaying around in the **current**, they look just like strands of seaweed. Since the leafy sea dragon looks nothing like a fish, a predator looking for food would completely ignore it.

Left This flounder is changing its color to blend in with its surroundings.

Below The leafy sea dragon looks like a clump of seaweed to its enemies.

7. Fooling the enemy

Some fish protect themselves by fooling predators that may wish to eat them. When attacking another fish, a predator aims just in front of its prey, hoping to catch it as it swims forward.

The threadfin butterfly fish confuses the predator by having patterns on its tail end, which look like a false eye and mouth. A predator is fooled into thinking that this is the head end of the fish. When it attacks this false head, the threadfin butterfly fish escapes by swimming off in the opposite direction.

A young twinspot wrasse also uses body markings to trick predators. On the sides of its body are two black and red spots, which look just like a pair of eyes. These make the whole body appear as one big face. A predator is afraid to attack what seems to be the head of a large fish.

The leatherjacket is not at all poisonous but escapes being eaten by imitating the very poisonous striped toby. No predator is likely to take a chance and eat what looks like a poisonous fish.

Below The black band on the head of this threadfin butterfly fish hides its eye.

Right From the side, a twinspot wrasse looks like the face of a large fish.

8. Difficult to swallow

The stonefish is the most poisonous fish there is. It has spines on its body that can inject deadly poisons into any fish that tries to eat it. Stonefish live in shallow **tropical** waters, and they look exactly like stones. This makes them very difficult to see. Anyone who is unlucky enough to step on a stonefish will be stung. The sting is very painful and can kill, but there is an antitoxin to treat it.

Imagine how hard it would be even for a big fish to swallow a soccer ball covered with sharp spines. This is the problem faced by any predator that tries to eat a porcupine fish. When alarmed, it makes itself much bigger and rounder by puffing its body up with water. As the porcupine fish inflates itself, the skin stretches and the spines stick out. If this happened in a predator's throat, the predator would be badly injured.

Sharks sometimes eat porcupine fish, but they have to deflate them with their very sharp teeth before swallowing.

Left This porcupine fish is fully inflated.

Below Stonefish are very hard to see.

9. Mating habits

Some people think that the oceans are silent. This is not true. Many sea animals, including some fish, make loud noises. Fish called croakers, or drumfish, which live around North America, make drumming and croaking noises to attract a mate. This noise is made by muscles in the fish's body, which vibrate like guitar strings. These vibrations are made louder by the **swim bladder**. The sounds are so loud that a fish 65 ft (20 m) down in the ocean can still be heard by a person in a boat above.

The male blue and gold angelfish is not content with just one mate but has a group of up to seven females. He fiercely defends his territory against other males that may try to sneak in and capture a female. He mates with all his females every day just before sunset.

When the male angelfish dies, an amazing thing happens. In a few hours, the biggest female of the group changes into a male and takes over where the dead male left off.

Below A blue and gold angelfish.

Right Drumfish make a very loud noise.

10. Baby care

The bitterling lives in European streams. It is one of the few fish that takes great care to make sure its young are safe after hatching. The female fish passes her eggs through a long tube from her body and lays them in a living freshwater mussel. The male bitterling then **fertilizes** the egg by releasing his **sperm** into the mussel as well. The mussel is used as a nursery for the young bitterlings for four weeks after they have hatched. During this time the young fish are protected from their enemies by the mussel's hard shell.

The brown discus fish is also a good parent. Both the male and the female allow their young to eat the mucus (clear slime) that covers the parents' bodies. When one parent has had enough of being nibbled, it will use its tail to flick the young fish to the other parent.

Left The egg tube of the female bitterling is entering a mussel.

Below Young discus fish eating the mucus on the parent's body.

11. Some good fathers

The male sea horse is an excellent parent. He looks after the 200 eggs that the female lays in his **brood pouch**. From two to six weeks later, tiny sea horses hatch inside the pouch. The "pregnant" father then spends the next two days giving birth. To steady himself during this time he grips a seaweed stem with his tail. As he bends his body backward and forward the babies pop out one at a time. They quickly swim to the surface for some air to fill their swim bladders.

Below This male sea horse has a full brood pouch.

Another very good parent is the male stickleback. He makes a nest for the eggs from little pieces of water weed. These are stuck together with a kind of glue that is made in his kidneys. By fanning water through the nest with his fins, he makes sure that the eggs have lots of **oxygen**. After hatching, the young sticklebacks emerge from the nest. If danger threatens, the male will suck the babies up and spit them back into the nest.

Right A male stickleback tending its nest before the female lays her eggs.

12. Useful friends

Some fish help others by cleaning them. One such fish is the cleaner wrasse. It spends a lot of its time in the mouths of larger fish removing **parasites** and pieces of waste food. The larger fish do not try to eat the cleaner wrasse, because cleaner wrasse are very important for keeping other fish healthy. When some scientists wanted to test this, they removed all the cleaner wrasse from a part of a reef. Several of the larger fish deserted that part of the reef, and the ones that remained became ill.

Left This cleaner wrasse is cleaning the gills of an angelfish.

Some fish help other animals too. One type of goby serves as a "lookout" for a certain type of shrimp. When a pair of these gobies are at the entrance to their burrow, the shrimp, which has very poor eyesight, keeps in touch with them with its long feelers. When danger threatens, the keen-sighted gobies flee down their burrow. The shrimp feels this movement and quickly follows.

In return for this warning the shrimp cleans and repairs the gobies' burrow.

Below The partnership between the goby and the shrimp works well.

13. Strange places to live

Some fish live in flooded caves where it is often completely dark. Fish living in these caves are born with perfect eyes, but their eyes gradually become useless, leaving the fish totally blind. Some cave fish eat insects that are washed into the cave with the flood water. Others eat bat droppings. The fish sense where the bat droppings are with their very sensitive taste-buds. These are found on the fish's lips as well as on its tongue. Although cave fish are swift swimmers, they manage to avoid bumping into things in the dark. They are able to detect where the obstacles are with their **lateral lines**.

Below Unlike any other fish, the strange-looking lungfish can breathe air.

Dry mud would seem a strange place to find a fish, but that is where the lungfish spends several months of the year.

The lungfish lives in South American, African, and Australian rivers. If these dry up in very hot weather, the lungfish burrows into the mud of the river bed until the river fills up with water again. The lungfish makes a cocoon around its body to keep moist while it is in the burrow. It is able to survive for many weeks or months in the mud by breathing air using its **lungs**.

It is very unusual for fish to have lungs. Most of them have gills to take oxygen from the water.

Right These cave fish have lost the use of their eyes and are totally blind.

GLOSSARY

Brood pouch A pocket-like swelling near the stomach of some fish where the fertilized eggs develop.

Coral reefs Formations in the sea that look like colorful, ragged rocks. They are actually made up of the hard skeletons deposited by certain sea creatures.

Current A flow or movement of water in an ocean, lake, or stream.

Dorsal fin The single fin on the back of a fish.

Fertilize When the male's sperm joins with the female's egg and causes it to develop into a young fish.

Gills The featherlike organs on fish that allow them to breathe under water.

Lateral line A line down each side of a fish that is used to sense vibrations in the water.

Lungs The organs air-breathing animals use to get oxygen.

Mangrove swamp A dense thicket of trees and shrubs growing in coastal areas.

Oxygen A very important gas that most living creatures need to breathe in order to live.

Parasites Plants or animals that live and feed on other plants or animals without being of any benefit to them.

Pectoral fins The two fins nearest to a fish's head.

Poison Any substance that, when taken into the body, causes harm or kills. Also called a *toxin*.

Predators Animals or fish that hunt and eat other animals or fish.

Prey Any animal or fish that is hunted for food.

School A large group of fish that swim or feed together.

Sperm The male reproductive cell.

Sponge A type of sea animal usually found near coral reefs that absorbs water.

Swim bladder An air-filled bag inside some fish. By altering the amount of air in the swim bladder a fish can make itself rise or sink in the water.

Tropical Of the areas just north and south of the Equator, which have very hot weather all year round.

Vertebrate An animal with a backbone.

FURTHER READING

A Look at Fish, by Kaye Quinn (Price
   Stern, 1986)
Hidden Under Water, by Kim Taylor
   (Delacorte, 1990)
Discovering Saltwater Fish, by Alwyne
   Wheeler (Bookwright, 1988)
Creatures of the Deep, by Lionel Bender
   (Gloucester Press, 1989)
Fish, by Louis Sabin (Troll Associates,
   1985)

Picture Acknowledgments

Biofotos/H. Angel 14, S. Summerhays 13; Bruce Coleman Ltd./J. Burton 10, 17, 21, 29,
K. Taylor 9, 22, 25, B. Wood 26; Frank Lane Picture Agency/R. Commer 7; NHPA 28;
OSF Ltd/M. Gibbs COVER, 5, 12, S. Hauser 12, R. H. Kuiter 15, 27; Z. Leszczynski 20;
Planet Earth/Seaphot Ltd/W. Deas 6, G. Douwma 24, P. Oliveira 23, C. Petron 18,
H. Vorgtman 4, N. Wu 8, 11; ZEFA/W. Townsend 12.

INDEX

Numbers in **bold** indicate photographs.